Sun and Moon

THIS EDITION
Editorial Management by Oriel Square
Produced for DK by WonderLab Group LLC
Jennifer Emmett, Erica Green, Kate Hale, *Founders*

Editors Grace Hill Smith, Libby Romero, Michaela Weglinski;
Photography Editors Kelley Miller, Annette Kiesow, Nicole DiMella;
Managing Editor Rachel Houghton; **Designers** Project Design Company;
Researcher Michelle Harris; **Copy Editor** Lori Merritt; **Indexer** Connie Binder;
Proofreader Larry Shea; **Reading Specialist** Dr. Jennifer Albro; **Curriculum Specialist** Elaine Larson

Published in the United States by DK Publishing
1745 Broadway, 20th Floor, New York, NY 10019

Copyright © 2023 Dorling Kindersley Limited
DK, a Division of Penguin Random House LLC
22 23 24 25 26 10 9 8 7 6 5 4 3 2 1
001-333849-May/2023

All rights reserved.

Without limiting the rights under the copyright reserved above, no part of this publication may be reproduced, stored in or introduced into a retrieval system, or transmitted, in any form, or by any means (electronic, mechanical, photocopying, recording, or otherwise), without the prior written permission of the copyright owner.
Published in Great Britain by Dorling Kindersley Limited

A catalog record for this book
is available from the Library of Congress.
HC ISBN: 978-0-7440-7091-0
PB ISBN: 978-0-7440-7092-7

DK books are available at special discounts when purchased in bulk for sales promotions, premiums,
fundraising, or educational use. For details, contact: DK Publishing Special Markets,
1745 Broadway, 20th Floor, New York, NY 10019
SpecialSales@dk.com

Printed and bound in China

The publisher would like to thank the following for their kind permission to reproduce their images:
a=above; c=center; b=below; l=left; r=right; t=top; b/g=background

Dorling Kindersley: NASA 8br; **Dreamstime.com:** Awargula 30cr, Fokusgood 6-7, Andrey Kotko / Raccoonn 11bl, Brian Kushner / Bkushner 22clb, Matthieuclouis 7c, Paulpaladin 8-9, Procyab 7bl, Chiew Ropram 24-25b, Jekaterina Sahmanova 9br, Smileus 10br, Nuttawut Uttamaharad 5tr; **Getty Images:** DigitalVision / Ariel Skelley 20br, Stone / Hans Neleman 5c; **NASA:** 28-29; **Shutterstock.com:** 19 STUDIO 23, Mihai_Andritoiu 20-21, Artsiom P 27cb, AstroStar 26-27, buradaki 6br, CandyRetriever 21bl, Castleski 28br, 29b, 31bl, herle_catharina 31cl, Mee Ko Dong 4crb, 12-13, 30crb, Elena11 27bl, EpicStockMedia 30, Juergen Faelchle 17cb, Graphics999 15b, LedyX 31tl, mapichai 19b, Nostalgia for Infinity 3clb, 26br, 31clb, Onkamon 3crb, 8cl, 30cra, otsphoto 11br, Photoartdesign 16br, Anurak Pongpatimet 30br, Redsapphire 24-25, Ricardo Reitmeyer 16-17, 31cla, SedmogJula10 13c, Aleksandra Suzi 5br, Johan Swanepoel 18-19, titoOnz 10-11, 14-15, TNK DESIGN 13bl, Peter Togel 9bl, Vibrant Image Studio 14br, Kayla Wolfe 4cr, XiXinXing 12br

Cover images: *Front:* **Dreamstime.com:** Valerii Brozhinskii, Yusuf Demirci br, Koryaba cra, Zeechinchun cl;
Shutterstock.com: Nostalgia for Infinity tr

All other images © Dorling Kindersley
For more information see: www.dkimages.com

For the curious
www.dk.com

Sun and Moon

Libby Romero

The Sun and the Moon are important to Earth. Let us learn why!

The Sun is a star.
The Sun is a hot ball of gas.

star

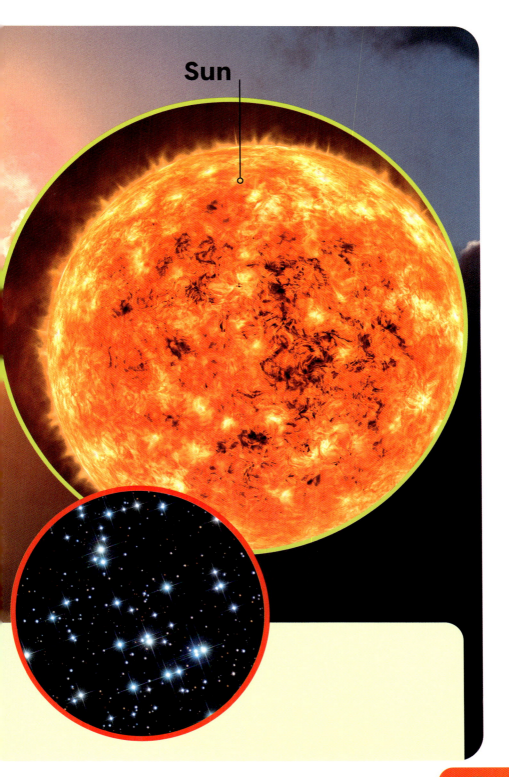
Sun

A moon is a dusty ball of rock.
Earth has one Moon.

Moon

moon

Earth

The Sun makes energy.

The Sun's energy goes to Earth as light and heat.

Sun's light

energy
[EH-ner-jee]

Plants and animals need light and heat to live.

live

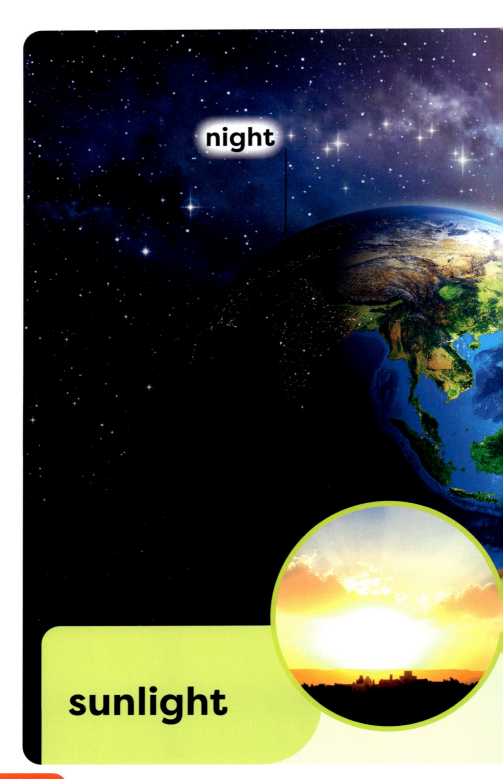

Sunlight shines on one side of Earth. Earth turns. Sunlight shines on the other side. That is why Earth has day and night.

day

Sunlight shines on the Moon. Light bounces off the Moon. That is why the Moon glows.

moon glow

Earth travels around the Sun.

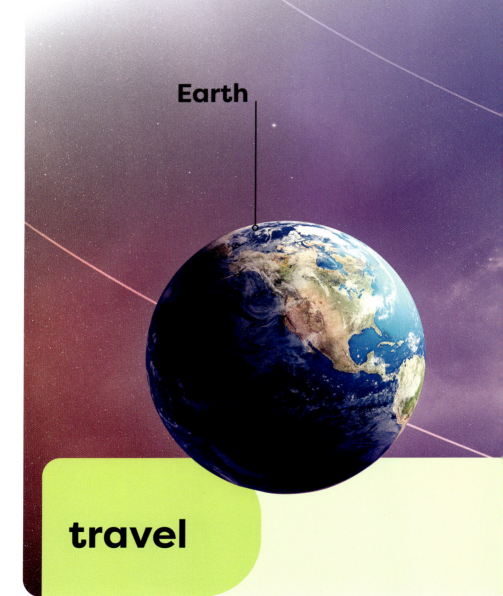

Earth

travel

Earth is tilted. The side leaning toward the Sun is hotter. That is why Earth has seasons.

seasons

21

The Moon moves
around Earth.
As it moves,
our view of
the Moon changes.

view of the moon

23

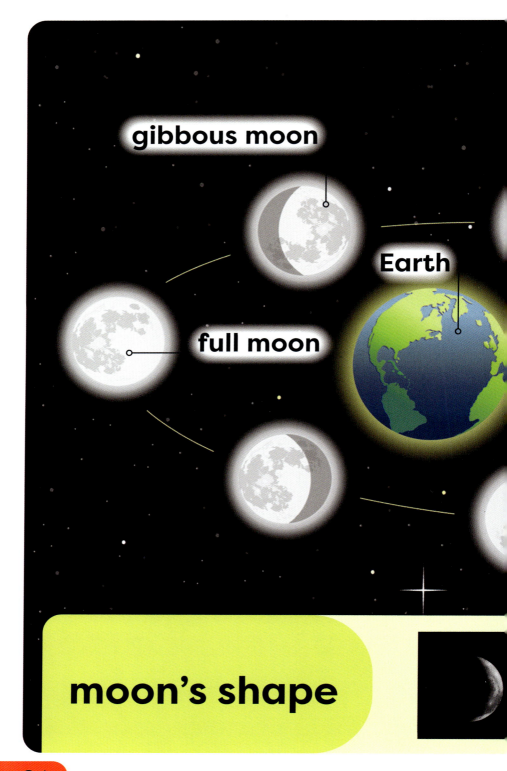

That is why the Moon looks like it changes shape.

People study the Sun and the Moon.
They use spacecraft.
They use telescopes.

spacecraft
[SPAYS-kraft]

26

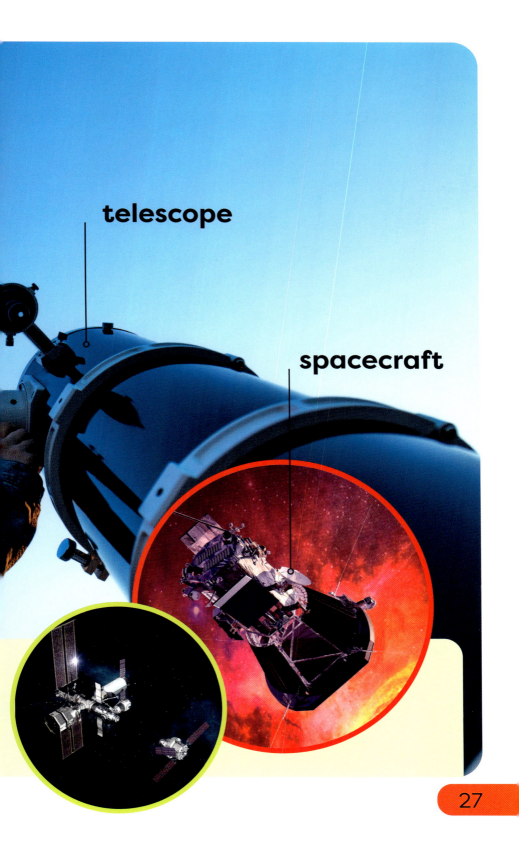

Astronauts have even gone to the Moon!

astronaut
[A-struh-NAAT]

Earth would not be the same without the Sun and the Moon.

Glossary

astronaut
a person trained to work and travel in outer space

energy
natural power; the ability to make something active

glow
a steady light

seasons
the four parts of the year: spring, summer, fall, and winter

spacecraft
a vehicle designed to travel in outer space

Quiz

Answer the questions to see what you have learned. Check your answers with an adult.

1. What does the Sun give to the Earth?

2. Why does the Moon glow?

3. Why does the Moon look like it changes shape?

4. What are two things people use to study the Sun and the Moon?

5. What do you think astronauts can learn by going to the Moon?

1. Light and heat 2. Sunlight bounces off the moon
3. Our view of the moon changes as it goes around Earth
4. Spacecraft and telescopes 5. Answers will vary